CLASSICAL GUITAR GEMS

BY

KEITH CALMES

The Corona model Madagascar Rosewood with Cedar Top guitar image on the cover is courtesy of Prenkert Guitars.

WWW.MELBAY.COM

Preface

Classical Guitar Gems is a diverse collection of excellent guitar music. A list of the composers says it best: Aguado, Bach, Beethoven, Carulli, Coste, Ruben Delgado, Emilia Giuliani, Justin Holland, Massenet, Pachelbel, Praetorius, Schumann, Tchaikovsky, Vivaldi, Waldteufel, and a traditional Colombian folk song. This book should provide welcome new repertoire for any classical guitarist.

Many of the pieces are works by well known composers for the guitar: Aguado, Carulli, and Coste. Some of the pieces are compositions for the guitar by somewhat lesser known composers: Emilia Giuliani (one of Mauro's daughters) and Ruben Delgado (a living composer and guitarist in California). The rest of the pieces in this collection are arrangements for the guitar from various sources. Most of the arrangements are mine. There is also an arrangement by Mel Bay (!) and another by Justin Holland (an African American pioneer of the instrument).

Care has been taken to provide guitarists with quality arrangements and fingerings.

It is a pleasure to share some of my favorite music with other classical guitarists and their audiences.

Keith Calmes

Contents

Study in A

Dionisio Aguado

Andantino

Study in e minor

Dionisio Aguado

Study in E

Dionisio Aguado

Andantino

Sinfonia

from the Cantata: Ich steh mit einem Fuß im Grabe (BWV 156)

J. S. Bach

Arr. by Keith Calmes

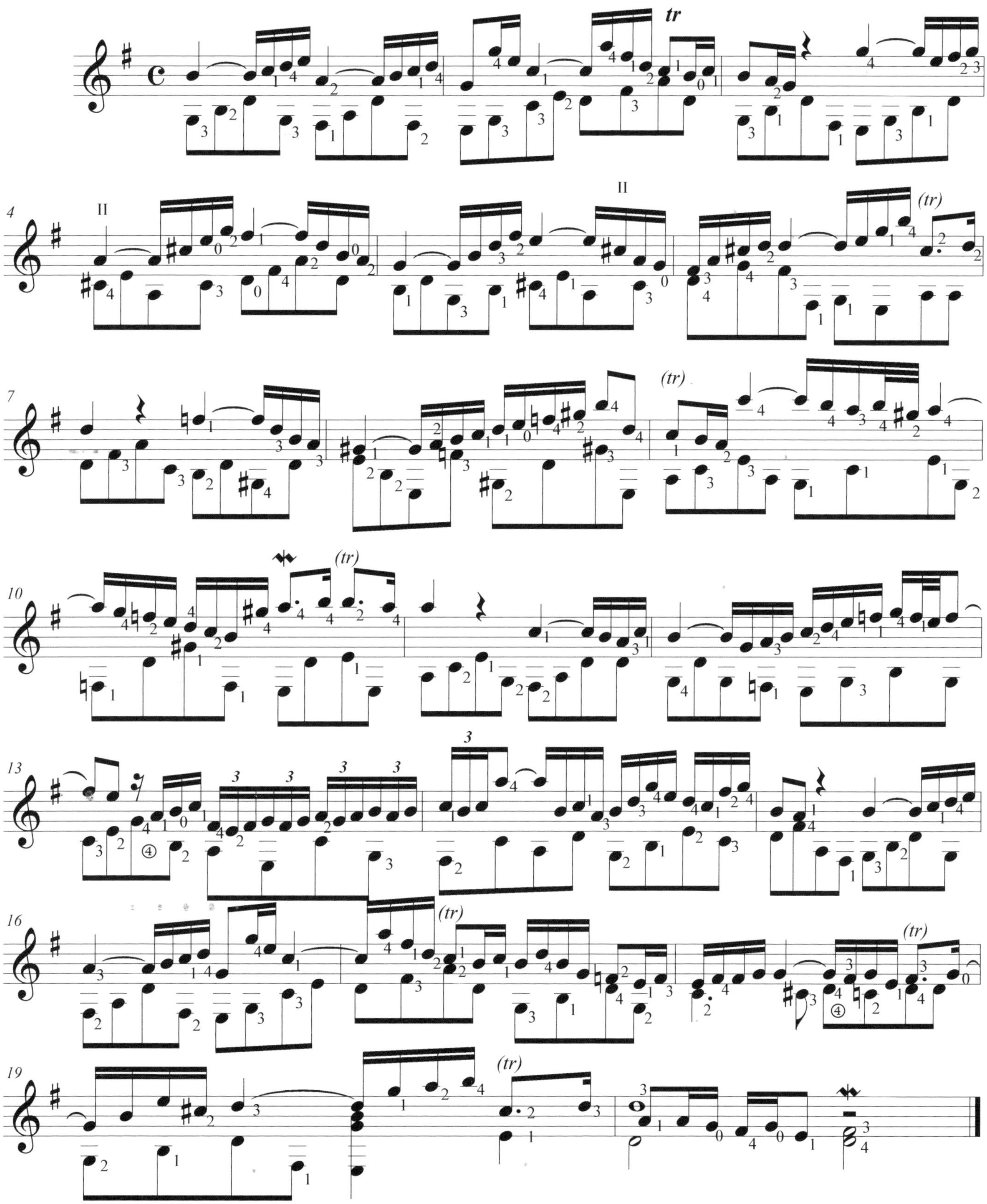

Für Elise

Ludwig van Beethoven

D.S. al Coda

Rondo

Ferdinando Carulli

Moderato

rall.
a tempo
VII
V
IX
p
sf

IX
p
cresc.
mf
V
III
1.
2.
D.S. al Coda
VIII
VIII

Barcarolle (Op. 51, #10)

Napoleon Coste

Menuet (Op. 51, #7)

Napolean Coste

Andante ♩ = 88

Rondeau (Op. 51, #6)

Napolean Coste

Rondoletto (Opus 51, #3)

Allegretto ♩ = 63

Napoleon Coste

This page has been left blank to avoid an awkward page turn.

Classical Dance

Ruben Delgado

66
1.
2.
74
82

Prelude in d minor

(Op. 46, #3)

Emilia Giuliani
All fingerings and articulation
are from the original publication.

Presto

VI

Pansy Blossom Waltz

Sidney Ryan
Arr. by Justin Holland
Fingerings and dynamics are from the original publication.

55
62
mf
69
76
83
90

Meditation
(from Thais)

Jules Massenet
Arr. by Keith Calmes

(hinge bar)

Canon

Johann Pachelbel
Arr. by Keith Calmes

(hinge bar)

Gilotte

Michael Praetorius
Arr. by Keith Calmes

Spagnoletta

Michael Praetorius
Arr. by Keith Calmes

A Chorale (Ein Choral)

(Op. 68, #4)

Robert Schumann
Arr. by Keith Calmes

First Loss (Erster Verlust)

(Op. 68, #16)

Robert Schumann

Arr. by Keith Calmes

Humming Song (TrallerLiedchen)

(Op. 68, #3)

Robert Schumann

Arr. by Keith Calmes

Melody
(Op. 68, #1)

Robert Schumann
Arr. by Keith Calmes

Nordic Song
(Op. 68, #41)

Robert Schumann
Arr. by Keith Calmes

Piece (Stückchen)
(Op. 68, #5)

Robert Schumann
Arr. by Keith Calmes

Dolores Waltz

Emile Waldteufel
Arr. by Mel Bay

Chanson Triste
(Op. 40, #2)

Pyotr Ilyich Tchaikovsky
Arr. by Keith Calmes

47
G
I
53
V
V
H
(hinge bar)
58
63

El Grillo
(The Cricket)

Traditional Columbian Folk Song

Arr. by Keith Calmes

33
X
38
VII
X
42
VII
① 5th fret
art. harm.

Largo

(from Concerto in D)

Antonio Vivaldi
Arr. by Keith Calmes

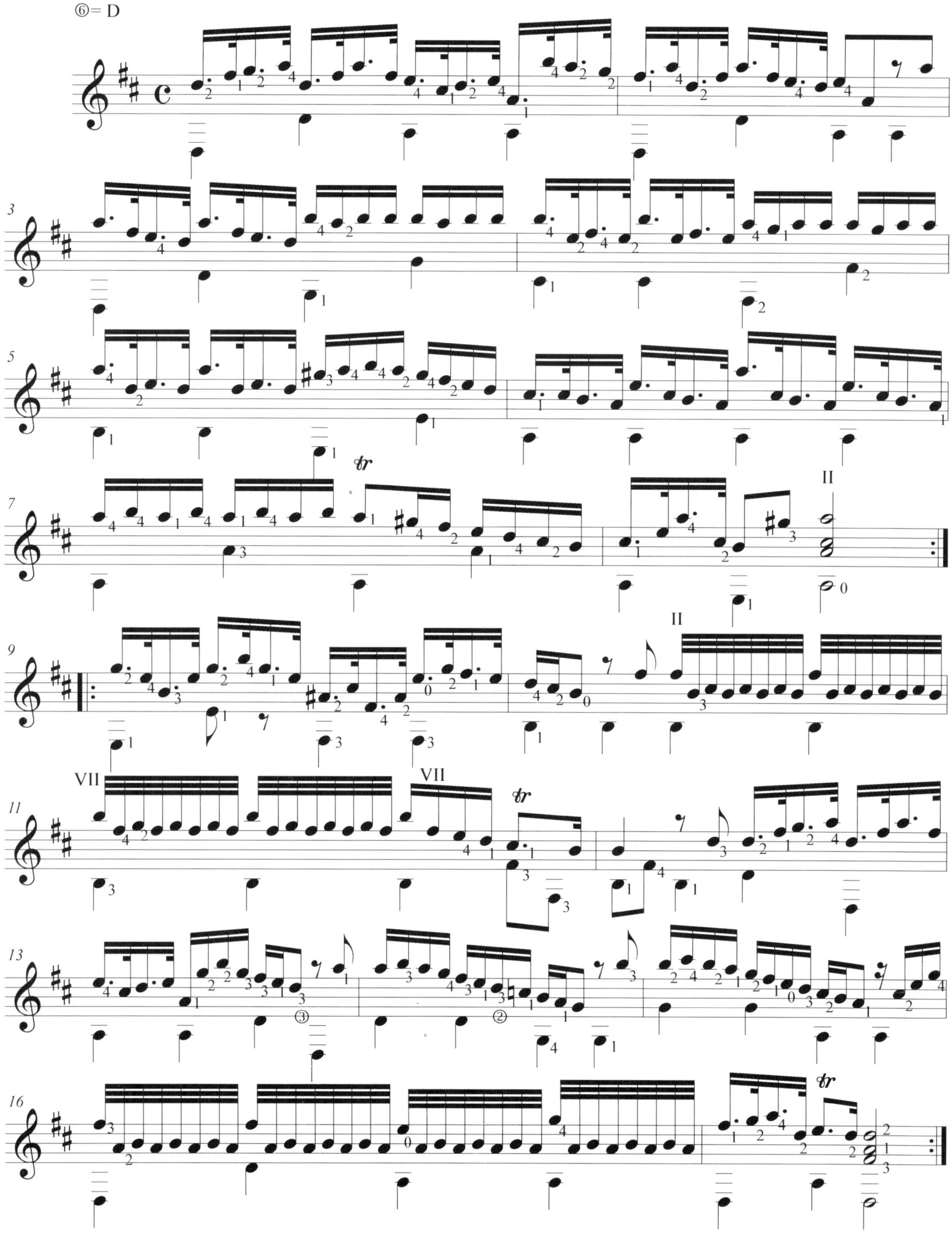

About the Author

Keith Calmes Photo credit: Joanna Patterson

Guitarist Keith Calmes earned degrees in Classical Guitar Performance at California State University Northridge, The Juilliard School, and University of Southern California. Keith has given lecture-recitals at the Saint Louis Art Museum, Mission San Luis in Florida, and at the national conventions of Guitar Foundation of America and American String Teachers Association. He gave his Carnegie Recital Hall debut as Winner of the Artists International Competition and has performed with guitarist Carlos Barbosa-Lima, Vikku Vinayakram (of Shakti) and his family band, and many others. Keith has released several other guitar books with Mel Bay Publications.

Other Mel Bay Classic Guitar Solo Books

6 Neapolitan Songs for Solo Classic Guitar (Scheldt)
A Dozen Italian Diversions for Guitar Solo (DiBenedetti)
Airs and Ballads for Classic Guitar (Lehmann-Haupt)
Arias for Acoustic Guitar: Operatic Melodies for Solo Guitar (Edwards)
Ashokan Farewell Guitar Arrangement (Ungar/Lehmann-Haupt)
Balkan Melodies for Classical Guitar (Miric)
Carmen Suite (Ausqui)
Civil War Suite for Classical Guitar (Brew)
Classical and Flamenco Guitar Solos and Etudes (Elysa Hochman/Jason Hochman)
Classic Guitar Tunes - Beautiful American Airs and Ballads (Miric)
Classic Guitar Tunes - English Folk Songs (Worley)
Classic Guitar Tunes - Fun Solos to Play (Calmes)
Classic Guitar Tunes - Gospel Favorites (Calmes)
Classic Guitar Tunes - Jigs and Reels (Munger)
Classic Guitar Tunes - O'Carolan Airs (Böger)
Classic Guitar Tunes - Songs of Faith (Middleton)
Classic Tangos (Halen)
Complete Works of Scott Joplin: 52 PIano Rags, Waltzes & Marches Transcribed for Guitar Solo (De Chiaro)
Contemporary Irish Music for Classic Guitar Solo (Feeley)
Favorite Hymns for Classical Guitar (Castle)
Five Popular Persian Ballads for Solo Guitar (Afshar)
Five Women Composers Arranged for Guitar (Newman)
Folk songs and Dances of the Jewish People for Acoustic Guitar (Back)
Early American Hymn Favorites for Classical Guitar (Miric)
Great American Marches, Polkas & Grand Concert Waltzes for Acoustic Guitar (Back)
Greek Traditional Music for Acoustic Guitar (Borjanic)
Irish Folk Songs for Classical Guitar (Marsh)
Joan Baez Suite for Solo Guitar (Duarte)
Melodies of the Far East for Guitar (Tuan Vu)
Nineteen Gilbert & Sullivan Favorites Arranged for Classical Guitar (Marrington)
O'Carolan Favorites for Classic Guitar (Böger)
O'Carolan for Classic Guitar (Böger)
Romantic Arias for Classical Guitar (Eckels)
Russian Folk Songs for Guitar Solo (Borjanic)
Solo Guitar Hymnal: Classic Guitar Solos for the Liturgical Calendar Year (Bass)
Stephen Foster for Classic Guitar (Böger)
Music of Debussy for Solo Guitar (Santos)
Turlough O'Carolan Irish Harp Pieces for Classic Guitar (Böger)
W. A. Mozart's "London Sketchbook" (Böger)
Wedding Favorites for Classical Guitar (De Chiaro)
Wedding Music for Classical Guitar (Boydston)